ISBN 979-8-35094-204-0

In memory of Joel

when you lose someone you love

it's like part of you is gone

it creates a huge hole inside you

you miss that person SO MUCH!

you are in pain

you feel sad and lonely

these are feelings of GRIEF

but you are not alone

there are people who love you

they are here for you

they will help you to fill this hole

they may come with different things

some people bring food

others come with flowers

...or a smile

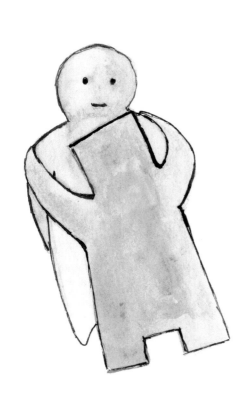

some come with a hug

... or kind words

...or big loving eyes

and others just want to spend time with you

there are people whose job is to help those

who are grieving

they will walk along with you and guide you

as you explore the different possible paths

in your journey

it's difficult to find your way through these

new paths and you may sometimes feel lost

don't be afraid to ask for help

among the people who are here for you

they are your "FOREVER" friends

they've always been there for you

some people may surprise you

you never thought

they would show up

but HERE they are!

they may become new friends

some have also lost a loved one

they REALLY understand your pain

you can even cry together

some people have lost the same person as you

they also have a big hole inside them

but everyone grieves differently

even if they have the same loss

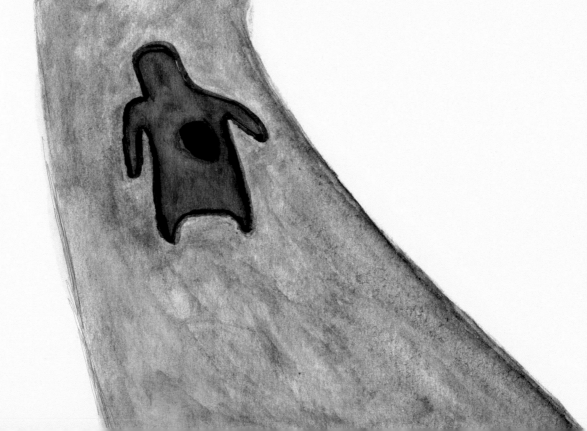

sometimes it's difficult for them to help you

and for you to help them

you both need to fill up your own hole first

before you can understand each other's pain

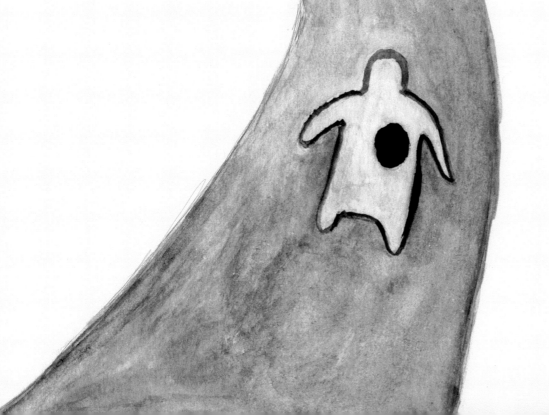

don't be too sad

some people you thought would be there

don't even show up

perhaps it's because they don't know what

to say or what to do

they may come to you later on

but eventually

one by one

all the people who love you

will fill up the hole that is inside you

it's like they each bring a piece of themselves

some bring a little piece

and some a BIG piece

and sometimes the tiniest piece

makes a HUGE difference

it may take a VERY LONG time

but at the end the hole is filled

you are still hurt

but the pain is not as deep

there is a legend that says it is the
person you have lost who glues the pieces
together so that this person will ALWAYS BE
PART OF YOU

at the end, all the pieces have different
shapes and colors and it may look irregular
and a bit awkward

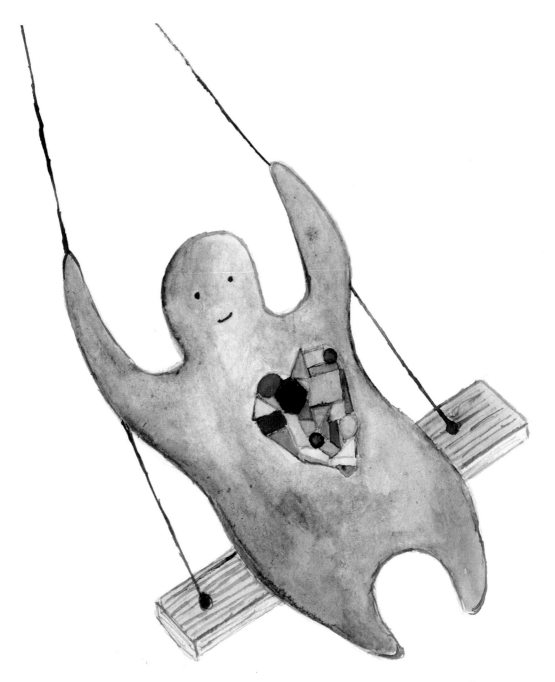

but it works! because it's made of LOVE

THANKS
to my family and my friends

thanks also to the different organizations that
have helped me through my journey
including:

JoAnn's bereavement group
MSK bereavement (Anastasia/Barbara)
Cancer Care (Cecilia)
Soaring Spirit (Richard's group)
Isolation Journal (Suleika)

you may use the page on the right to write the

names of all the people who have come to help

you fill your hole of grief